THE AUDUBON SOCIETY POCKET GUIDES

A Chanticleer Press Edition

Kenneth D. Heil
Associate Professor and Curator of Herbarium
San Juan College

Richard Spellenberg, consultant
Professor of Biology
New Mexico State University

FAMILIAR CACTI

Alfred A. Knopf, New York

Contents

Introduction
How to Use This Guide 6
Identifying Cacti 9
Habitat Types 12
Parts of a Cactus 15

The Cacti 18

Appendices
Guide to Genera 178
Glossary 185
Index 187
Credits 191

How to Use This Guide

One of the most versatile families of plants, cacti have adapted to survive under conditions that would destroy most other plants, and even most animals, within a matter of hours. They have unique shapes, are usually well armed with sharp spines, and produce flowers that are among the most beautiful in the plant kingdom. Besides being a favorite among landscapers, cacti are enjoyable to find and identify in their natural environments. They are New World plants, occurring from northern Canada to near the tip of South America. In the United States, cacti are found from the moist tropics of Florida to the driest deserts of California. These spiny plants grow in every state except Alaska, Hawaii, Maine, New Hampshire, and Vermont. Texas has the highest number of different kinds of cacti, followed by Arizona, New Mexico, and California. Cacti are also common in Utah, Nevada, Colorado, and Florida. Outside of North America, cacti are now found in many of the warmer parts of the world.

Coverage This guide covers 80 of the most common and interesting cacti found in North America. Some rare cacti that are found only in a few locations are also discussed. To broaden the scope of this book, varieties and additional, similar or related species are mentioned.

Organization	This easy-to-use pocket guide is divided into three parts: introductory essays, illustrated accounts of the cacti, and appendices.
Introduction	As a basic introduction, the essay "Identifying Cacti" offers useful information about which features to notice in looking at these plants. A special section called "Habitat Types" defines terms commonly used to describe various areas where cacti are found, listing geographic location, elevation, and conspicuous vegetation to help you confirm your identification. This is followed by a series of black-and-white drawings that illustrate the different parts of cactus plants.
The Cacti	This section contains 80 color plates arranged visually, according to stem shape. The pages facing the photographs present text accounts of the species. Each begins with an introductory paragraph that gives interesting facts and lore and describes similar species and varieties. Next comes a description of the most important characteristics of the cactus, followed by information about its habitat and geographical range. Ranges are described using the names of states as well as those of deserts where relevant. A black-and-white drawing representing the plant's genus supplements the photograph.

Appendices	To help you recognize the various types of cacti, "A Guide to Genera" describes the basic characteristics of each genus covered in this book. A black-and-white drawing of a representative species is included in each description, along with a page reference to the related text accounts. Also included are a glossary of commonly used terms and an index.
A Word of Caution	Unfortunately, the populations of many native cacti have been seriously depleted as a result of land development, construction, and grazing, among other intrusions. Many states have passed laws protecting cacti, and heavy fines can result from the illegal collection of these plants. Some cacti are federally protected by the Endangered Species Act of 1973. If you plan to landscape with cacti, it is prudent to buy plants or seeds from reputable nurseries, and leave these splendid plants to thrive in their natural habitats.

Identifying Cacti

You will learn to identify many cacti by paying attention to four features: where a cactus grows (its habitat and range), the characteristics of its stem or stems, the types, number, and color of its spines, and the appearance of its flowers.

Location

You can narrow down the number of possible identities of a cactus by simply noting where it is found. Is it growing in the Mojave Desert, the Great Plains grassland, or an Eastern deciduous forest? Is it located on a hillside or on the flats? Does it grow in sandy soils or limestone outcrops? Many cacti will thrive only in particular habitats. If you think you have identified a cactus using the color plates in this book, but you find that the range description given does not apply, chances are that you are incorrect. However, the plant you have found may be a close relative (or possibly a variety) of the cactus described.

Stems

Cactus stems vary in height from thirty-five feet or more, like those of the tree-size Saguaro, to only about one and a half inches, like those of Knowlton's Cactus. Photosynthesis occurs in the stems of cacti. Cacti stems are succulent, meaning they are fleshy and serve as reservoirs for water. Many cacti stems swell during the wet season and shrink during the dry season, causing the plant's appearance to change considerably.

Areoles, Spines, and Glochids Areoles, unique to cacti, are the regions where the spines originate. Not all cacti have spines, but all cacti do have areoles.

The sharp spines protect the plant from browsers, provide some shade, and help direct water to the base of the plant, where it can be absorbed by the roots. Spine characteristics are very important in identifying a cactus. Many cacti have spines that all look alike, as do the prickly pears, but some cacti have both central and radial spines. Central spines originate at or near the center of the areole, are usually wide at the base, and vary in number from species to species. Radial spines radiate from the central spines like the spokes of a wheel; they also vary in number.

Glochids are sharp, minute, barbed bristles or hairs found only in prickly pears and chollas. They can be a painful nuisance to the unwary collector who tries to grab such cacti.

Flowers The blooms of plants in the cactus family are some of the most spectacular found among all flowering plants. They arise in the areole, have an inferior ovary, many stamens, and numerous sepaloid and petaloid perianth parts.

Fruits The fruits of most cacti are juicy and fleshy. They may contain spines or scales, and some are edible. Birds and rodents often eat cacti fruit and are therefore very important in seed dispersal.

The drawings on page 15 illustrate the various parts of a cactus.

Habitat Types	Following are descriptions of habitats where cacti typically grow.
Rocky Mountain Montane Forest	Idaho south to Arizona and New Mexico. 2,000–9,000 feet elevation. Indicator plants: douglas-fir, ponderosa pine, and Rocky Mountain juniper.
Pacific Montane Forest	Washington south to Baja California. 5,000–7,000 feet elevation. Indicator plants: ponderosa pine, sugar pine, and white fir.
Juniper-Pinyon Woodlands	Columbia Basin; western Texas, New Mexico, northern Arizona, southern and northwestern Colorado, and southern Utah. 5,000-7,000 feet elevation. Indicator plants: Utah juniper, oneseed juniper, one- and two-needle pinyon pines.
Sagebrush Community	Columbia Basin; Utah and Nevada. 4,000-6,000 feet elevation. Indicator plants: big sagebrush and saltbushes.
Eastern Deciduous Forest	Gulf of Mexico, Atlantic coast, and Great Lakes region. Sea level to 2,000 feet elevation. Indicator plants: dogwood, white and red oaks, magnolia, basswood, and sugar maple.
Great Plains Grassland	North Dakota and eastern Montana south to eastern New

Mexico and northern Texas. 3,000-6,000 feet elevation. Indicator plants: numerous grasses.

Palouse Prairie — Eastern Washington, eastern Oregon, and adjacent Idaho. 2,000-2,500 feet elevation. Indicator plants: numerous grasses.

Desert Grassland — Southeastern Arizona, southwestern New Mexico, and Trans-Pecos Texas. 2,500-5,000 feet elevation. Indicator plants: numerous grama grasses.

Edwards Plateau — Central Texas. 2,000-3,000 feet elevation. Indicator plants: numerous oaks and mesquite.

Rio Grande Plain — Along the Rio Grande in Texas. Sea level to 1,000 feet elevation. Indicator plants: numerous oaks, mesquite, and prickly pear cactus.

Oak Woodlands — Arizona, southwestern New Mexico, California, and southwestern Oregon. Near sea level to 6,000 feet elevation. Indicator plants: numerous oaks, pinyon pine and California buckeye.

California Chaparral — Southern California. 1,000-5,000 feet elevation. Indicator plants: manzanita, mountain lilac, and currant.

Caribbean Tropical Forest — Southern tips of Florida and Texas. Near sea level.

Indicator plants: fig, strangler fig, black mangrove, and catclaw.

Navajoan Desert   The Four Corners region of the Colorado plateau. Northeastern Arizona, southwestern Colorado, northwestern New Mexico, and southeastern Utah. 4,000–5,000 feet elevation. Indicator plants: sagebrush and blackbrush.

Mojave Desert   Northwestern Arizona, southwestern Utah, southern tip of Nevada, and adjacent California. Near sea level to 4,000 feet elevation. Indicator plants: Joshua tree, desert crucifixion thorn, Mormon tea, and indigo bush.

Sonoran Desert   California and southern Arizona. 1,500–3,500 feet elevation. Indicator plants: California palm, smoke tree, diamond cholla, wolf berry, saguaro, palo verde, desert broom, and bur sage.

Chihuahuan Desert   Southern New Mexico and Trans-Pecos Texas. 4,000–6,000 feet elevation. Indicator plants: lechuguilla, bear grass, desert willow, and desert crucifixion thorn.

Parts of a Cactus

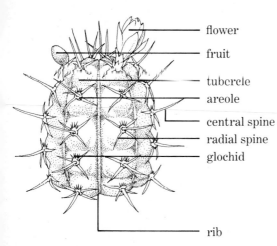

- flower
- fruit
- tubercle
- areole
- central spine
- radial spine
- glochid
- rib

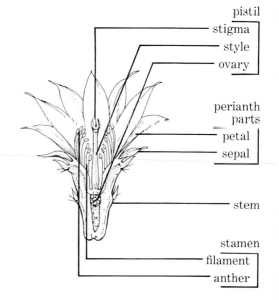

pistil
- stigma
- style
- ovary

perianth parts
- petal
- sepal

- stem

stamen
- filament
- anther

THE CACTI

Lemon Vine *Pereskia aculeata*

Although the Lemon Vine's broad, flat leaves make it look more like a thorny bush than a cactus, and it is found in junglelike woods rather than in the arid Southwest, it is a member of the cactus family. *Pereskia* is presumed to be rather primitive, retaining characteristics that cacti possessed before they adapted to dry habitats. Most photosynthesis of *Pereskia* takes place in its leaves, but this plant does have the areoles and spines characteristic of the cactus family. *Pereskia grandiflora,* another species found in Florida, reaches tree size. The Lemon Vine blooms from June to July.

Identification Clambering vines with broad, flat leaves. Leaves 2¾″ long; 1½″ wide. 1–7 spines, straight. Flowers white to pink; 1–1¾″ wide.

Habitat Woods and thickets of the tropical forest.

Range Southern Florida.

Silver Cholla *Opuntia echinocarpa*

Because the spine color varies from silvery to straw-yellow to golden in different populations of this cactus, it is also called the Golden Cholla. It is one of the most common of nearly two dozen chollas in the Southwest, many of which are difficult to identify because there is often hybridization among each type. The Silver Cholla varies in size from a short shrub to a very small tree. Two varieties, *echinocarpa* and *wolfii*, are recognized. Var. *echinocarpa* is very common but not as robust as the spiny, low-growing var. *wolfii*. The Silver Cholla blooms in May.

Identification   Many-branched shrub, mostly 3½–5′ tall. Terminal joint length: mostly 2-6″; terminal joint width: ¾″. 3–12 spines. Flowers yellowish green with streaks of red; 1¼–1¾″ long; 1¼–2¼″ wide.

Habitat   Sandy or gravelly soils of hillsides, ledges, mesas, flats, and washes.

Range   Southern Nevada, extreme southwestern Utah, southern California, and western Arizona. Mojave and Sonoran deserts.

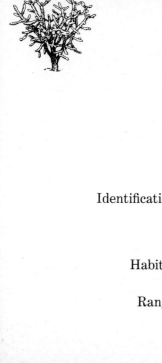

Buckhorn Cholla *Opuntia acanthocarpa*

The Buckhorn Cholla is often found growing in the same range as the Silver Cholla, and sometimes it is not easy to tell them apart. The Silver Cholla usually has one main trunk and a tubercle length one to two times the width. The Buckhorn Cholla usually has several small trunks and a tubercle length three to several times the width. The Buckhorn Cholla is often quite shrubby, but some plants are treelike and reach up to 13 feet tall. The flower buds are sometimes steamed and used as food by the Pima Indians. Up to five varieties of Buckhorn Cholla have been described. The delicate flowers bloom from May to June.

Identification Many-branched shrub to small tree, mostly 3½–13′ tall. Terminal joint length: 4¾–20″; terminal joint width: ¾–1½″. 6–25 spines. Flowers yellow, or red to purple; 1¼–1¾″ long; 1–2″ wide.

Habitat Sandy or gravelly soils of hillsides, ledges, mesas, flats, and washes.

Range Southern tip of Nevada, extreme southwestern Utah, southern California, and southern and western Arizona. Mojave and Sonoran deserts.

22

Rat-tail Cholla *Opuntia whipplei*

The Rat-tail Cholla is a low cactus that forms dense, spiny thickets, making it a pest to domestic livestock grazing on rangelands. In the spring this rather ragged-looking cactus is briefly showy, as its bright yellow to green flowers are displayed. The Rat-tail Cholla is a hardy cold-desert dweller that grows at elevations of 3,500–8,000 feet. Var. *whipplei* is quite common and widespread, while a few populations of var. *multigeniculata* grow in the Mojave Desert. Var. *viridiflora* is rare, known only from near Santa Fe, New Mexico. The Rat-tail Cholla blooms from late May to June.

Identification   Mat-forming or erect shrub, mostly 1–2′ tall. Terminal joint length: 1½–6″; terminal joint width: ½–¾″. 4–12 spines, white to yellow. Flowers green tinged with red, or lemon-yellow to pale yellow; 1¼–1½″ long; ¾–1¼″ wide.

Habitat   Hillsides, flats, and plains in desert grasslands and pinyon-juniper woodlands.

Range   Southern tip of Nevada, southeastern and southwestern Utah, southwestern Colorado, northern Arizona, and northwestern New Mexico. Great Basin and Mojave deserts.

24

Tree Cholla *Opuntia imbricata*

This cactus is one of the easternmost tree cholla types. Some "old-timers" reach 6½ feet tall and certainly deserve the name Tree Cholla, but other plants are shorter, thicket-forming shrubs. *O. spinosior* is a closely related species common in southeastern Arizona and southwestern New Mexico. Its tubercles measure ½" to ¾" long, while those of the Tree Cholla measure ¾" to 1½". They both bloom in late May and June.

Identification   Small tree or shrub, mostly 3–6½′ tall. Terminal joint length: 5–15″; terminal joint width: ¾–1¼″. 10–30 spines. Flowers red to magenta; 2–2½″ long; 2–3″ wide.

Habitat   Sandy or gravelly soils of hillsides, flats, mesas, and grasslands.

Range   Southeastern Colorado, southeastern Arizona, New Mexico, northern and western Texas, Oklahoma panhandle, extreme southwestern Kansas, and Great Plains grasslands. Chihuahuan Desert.

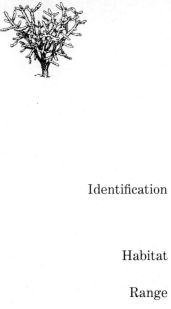

Jumping Cholla *Opuntia fulgida*

Be sure to watch where you step when entering a forest of Jumping Cholla. If you don't, the barbed, spiny stems may "jump" and cling to your boots. A few steps later, you may find the spines embedded in the back of your leg. This cactus is most easily recognized by its chains of fruits, which look like clusters of large, knobby, greenish grapes. The fruits remain on the plant and produce new flowers, giving rise in subsequent years to chains of fruit. The straw-colored spines are also quite attractive. Jumping Cholla usually blooms in June.

Identification   Small trees up to 14′ tall. The trunk branches and rebranches. Terminal joint length: 2–6″; terminal joint width: 1¼–2″. 6–12 spines. Flowers pink; approximately 1″ long and wide.

Habitat   Sandy and gravelly soils of hillsides, mesas, flats, and washes.

Range   Southcentral and southwestern Arizona. Sonoran Desert.

Teddy-bear Cholla *Opuntia bigelovii*

Don't let the name Teddy-bear Cholla mislead you—this cactus is anything but cuddly. Its stubby, more or less ovoid branches look like the arms and legs of a teddy bear. It is also short in stature and fuzzy-looking from a distance; a group of *O. bigelovii* can resemble an army of teddy bears marching up a hot, arid hillside. Because the spines are barbed and extremely sharp, it is a painful task to pull off a branch of this cholla once it has become embedded in your skin. Don't try to extract it with your fingers, or they will become stuck too. If the stem is not too deeply embedded, brace the stem between two hair combs and pull quickly; otherwise, cut off each spine with scissors. The Teddy Bear Cholla blooms in May and June.

Identification	Short trees, mostly 4′ but up to 8′ tall. Several short lateral branches. Terminal joint length: mostly 3–5″; terminal joint width: 1½–2½″. 6–10 spines. Flowers pale green or yellow; 1–1½″ long and wide.
Habitat	Gravelly hillsides and flats.
Range	Southeastern California to southcentral Arizona. Sonoran Desert.

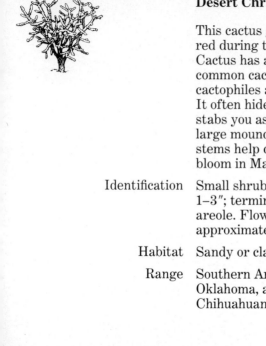

Desert Christmas Cactus *Opuntia leptocaulis*

This cactus gets its name from its fruits, which turn bright red during the winter months. The Desert Christmas Cactus has a very wide range and is one of the most common cacti in the southwestern United States. Most cactophiles and ranchers consider it a widespread pest. It often hides in a mesquite, or some other shrub, and stabs you as you walk by. This shrubby cholla often forms large mounds covered with spines, and its pencil-thin stems help distinguish it from other chollas. The flowers bloom in May.

Identification   Small shrub, mostly 1–2′ tall. Terminal joint length: 1–3″; terminal joint width: mostly ¼″. 1 spine per areole. Flowers yellowish green to bronze; ½–¾″ long; approximately ¾″ wide.

Habitat   Sandy or clay soils of flats, valleys, and bottomlands.

Range   Southern Arizona, southern New Mexico, southern Oklahoma, and Texas. Mojave, Sonoran, and Chihuahuan deserts.

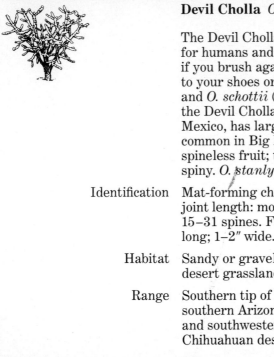

Devil Cholla *Opuntia stanlyi*

The Devil Cholla often forms mats that are impenetrable for humans and animals. Its spines are heavily barbed, so if you brush against the plant, the stems dislodge and stick to your shoes or clothing. *Opuntia clavata* (Club Cholla) and *O. schottii* (Dog Cholla) are two close relatives of the Devil Cholla. The Club Cholla, found in central New Mexico, has larger, daggerlike spines. The Dog Cholla, common in Big Bend National Park in Texas, has spineless fruit; the fruit of the Devil Cholla is usually spiny. *O. stanlyi* blooms in May.

Identification   Mat-forming cholla up to several feet wide. Terminal joint length: mostly 3–6″; terminal joint width: ½–1¾″. 15–31 spines. Flowers yellow or, rarely, reddish; 2–3″ long; 1–2″ wide.

Habitat   Sandy or gravelly soils of plains, valleys, and flats in desert grasslands.

Range   Southern tip of Nevada, southeastern California, southern Arizona, extreme southwestern New Mexico, and southwestern Texas. Mojave, Sonoran, and Chihuahuan deserts.

34

Diamond Cholla *Opuntia ramosissima*

Diamond-shaped tubercles and long tan spines are distinctive features of the Diamond Cholla. This old veteran seems to thrive in extremely arid climates. Most plants are shrublike, although some reach almost tree size. All Diamond Chollas branch profusely, and shorter ones may even form thickets. Some of the tallest Diamond Chollas have been found in Joshua Tree National Monument, California. The attractive flowers bloom in May.

Identification   Small tree or shrub, mostly ½–5′ tall. Terminal joint length: 2–4″; terminal joint width: approximately ¼″. 1–3 spines per areole. Flowers yellow to brown; 1¼–1¾″ long; approximately ½″ wide.

Habitat   Sandy soils of flats and washes.

Range   Southern tip of Nevada, southeastern California, and western Arizona. Mojave and Sonoran deserts.

Plains Prickly Pear *Opuntia polyacantha*

There are close to two dozen species of prickly pears found throughout the United States. Like the chollas, they are often difficult to distinguish due to hybridization. *O. polyacantha* is one of the most variable of the prickly pear cacti. Its distinctive characteristics include fruit that is tan and dry and a pad length reaching five inches. The Plains Prickly Pear blooms in May and June.

Identification Mat- or clump-forming prickly pear reaching several feet wide and 3–6″ tall. Terminal joint length: mostly 2–4″; terminal joint width: 1–4″. 4–10 spines. Flowers yellow or rose to deep red; 1¾–3″ long; 1¾–3¼″ wide.

Habitat Sandy or gravelly soils of hillsides, flats, canyon rims, and woodlands in pine forests; pinyon-juniper woodlands; sagebrush flats; grasslands; montane forests; and deserts.

Range Southwestern and southcentral Canada; southwestern Washington, northeastern Oregon, and adjacent Idaho north to the Dakotas; Utah, Colorado, southeastern California, northern Arizona, New Mexico, Oklahoma panhandle, and southwestern Texas. Great Basin, Mojave, and Sonoran deserts.

Brittle Cactus *Opuntia fragilis*

The Brittle Cactus, a low-growing, mat-forming cactus with a very wide distribution, is the northernmost cactus in North America. It is one of three that cross the border into Canada. The Brittle Cactus is most easily recognized by its small stems, which readily detach, its strongly barbed spines, and its dry fruit. It blooms in June.

Identification Mat-forming prickly pear up to several feet wide. Terminal joint length: ¾–1¾"; terminal joint width: ½–1". 1–6 spines. Flowers yellow to yellowish green; 1¼–1½" long; 1½–1¾" wide.

Habitat Sandy or gravelly soils of hillsides, plains and valleys in montane forests, pinyon-juniper woodlands, sagebrush deserts, and grasslands.

Range Western and central Canada, Washington, Oregon, Idaho, Montana, and the Dakotas; eastern Wyoming, western Nebraska, extreme northern California, extreme northeastern Nevada, Utah, Colorado, Kansas, Arizona, northern New Mexico, and panhandles of Oklahoma and Texas. Great Plains grasslands, Rocky Mountain montane forests, and Great Basin Desert.

Beavertail Cactus *Opuntia basilaris*

Although the Beavertail Cactus is spineless, you shouldn't handle it because it does have numerous microscopic, barbed spines called glochids. These glochids release from the pad at the slightest touch and become firmly embedded in the skin. The stems resemble a beaver's tail and are often deep purple. The flowers are delicate and showy, ranging in color from rose to magenta, and the fruit is fleshy. This cactus blooms from late February to early June.

Identification Low-growing prickly pear up to 1′ tall and 6′ wide. Terminal joint length: mostly 2–8″; terminal joint width: 1–6″. 1–5 spines found only in var. *treleasei.* Flowers range from rose to magenta; 2–3″ long and wide.

Habitat Sandy or gravelly soils of canyons, canyon rims, hillsides, and flats of grassland communities, oak woodlands, chaparral, pinyon-juniper woodlands, and sagebrush deserts.

Range Southern Nevada, extreme southwestern Utah, southern California, and western Arizona. Great Basin, Mojave, and Sonoran deserts.

Creeping Cactus *Opuntia pusilla*

In some parts of the eastern United States swimmers, beachcombers, and others who go barefoot must beware of this inconspicuous little cactus. It is usually found on sand dunes above the beaches, where it forms mats with stems containing strongly barbed, sharp spines. It is easily recognized by its mat-forming tendencies and joints that readily detach. The fleshy fruit rarely produces seed. Creeping Cactus blooms from June to July.

Identification   Mat-forming, creeping prickly pear up to 3″ tall. Terminal joint length: 1–2″; terminal joint width: ½–1″. Usually 1 spine per areole. Flowers bright yellow; 1¾–2½″ long and wide.

Habitat   Sandy soils near coastal areas.

Range   Coastal regions of southeastern Texas, east to North Carolina, and south to Florida.

Eastern Prickly Pear *Opuntia humifusa*

The Eastern Prickly Pear grows best in the eastern half of the United States, where it receives more rainfall than it would in the Southwest. It is often inconspicuous, growing among other vegetation in sandy or rocky habitats. It may form clumps or mats, and often forms hybrids with other prickly pear types. The Eastern Prickly Pear is most easily recognized by its fleshy fruit and needlelike spines. The Eastern Prickly Pear blooms from June to July.

Identification Mat- or clump-forming prickly pear up to 4″ high. Terminal joint length: mostly 2–4½″; terminal joint width: mostly 1½–3½″. 0–1 spines per areole. Flowers yellow; 1½–2¼″ long and wide.

Habitat Sandy or rocky soils of hillsides, valleys, and near shorelines in grasslands and eastern deciduous forests.

Range Eastern Texas north to eastern Iowa, and the remainder of the eastern United States except Maine.

Sprawling Prickly Pear *Opuntia littoralis*

The Sprawling Prickly Pear is often found in huge colonies, its glistening red fruits contrasting with its yellow-green stems. It is most common in southwestern California, where it usually dwells in the California chaparral. Cochineal insects often feed on the Sprawling Prickly Pear and a relative, *Opuntia ficus-indica* (Indian Fig). The female insect produces a red dye that is used by southern Indians for staining fabrics. The Sprawling Prickly Pear blooms in May and June.

Identification Sprawling prickly pear up to 2' high and several feet wide. Terminal joint length: mostly 3–10"; terminal joint width: mostly 3–4". 1–11 spines. Flowers waxy yellow, yellow with red center, or vivid red to magenta; 2–3" long and wide.

Habitat Sandy or rocky soils of hillsides, beaches, washes, alluvial fans, and bluffs in the chaparral, deserts, pinyon-juniper woodlands, and montane forests.

Range Southern Nevada, extreme southern Utah, southern California, and northern Arizona. Great Basin and Mojave deserts.

Purple Prickly Pear *Opuntia macrocentra*

The vivid color of the Purple Prickly Pear's stems is caused by a pigment that helps protect it from harsh sun and extremely hot temperatures. Striking black spines contrast sharply with its purple stems, making the Purple Prickly Pear one of the handsomest species found in the southwestern deserts. Var. *macrocentra* is one of several varieties that have been described. It usually has one to two spines that are two to five inches long and is common in Big Bend National Park in Texas. Var. *santa rita*, which has no spines, is common in the Tucson, Arizona, region. The Purple Prickly Pear blooms from April to June.

Identification	Sprawling or treelike prickly pear. Terminal joint length and width: 4–8″. 1–4 spines. Flower petals yellow with red bases; 3–3½″ long and wide.
Habitat	Sandy or gravelly soils of hillsides, flats and washes in deserts and desert grasslands.
Range	Southern Arizona east to southern New Mexico, and southwestern Texas. Sonoran and Chihuahuan deserts.

New Mexico Prickly Pear   *Opuntia phaeacantha*

The New Mexico Prickly Pear is an erect or sprawling shrub with fleshy fruit and brown to black spines. This species has a very wide range, and up to ten or more varieties have been described, making exact identification confusing. Usually the varieties are distinguished by pad size, spine distribution on the pad, spine color and size, and fruit length. The New Mexico Prickly Pear has adapted to both the deserts of Texas and the cool, moist forests of the Rocky Mountains. It blooms from April to June.

Identification   Sprawling or erect prickly pear up to 3′ tall and several feet wide. Terminal joint length: 5–8″; terminal joint width: 3–6″. 1–8 spines. Flowers yellow to orange with bright red centers; 2–3″ long and wide.

Habitat   Sandy or gravelly soils of hillsides, flats, canyon rims, and mesas in grasslands, deserts, oak woodlands, chaparral, pinyon-juniper woodlands, and montane forests.

Range   Southern Nevada, Utah, Colorado, southern California, Arizona, New Mexico, western Kansas, Oklahoma, and the western two-thirds of Texas. Great Basin, Mojave, and Chihuahuan deserts.

Engelmann Prickly Pear *Opuntia engelmannii*

This is another variable and wide-ranging prickly pear found in the southwestern deserts. The Engelmann Prickly Pear is a tough pioneer, often thriving in regions where other plants can't grow. Its rich burgundy fruits are edible and quite juicy. In Mexico the fruits, or *tunas,* are a major food, commonly sold in markets and at roadside stands. When served chilled, they are refreshingly sweet. *Tunas* are now also common in Old World markets in arid lands. The Engelmann Prickly Pear blooms from late April to June.

Identification Shrub-size prickly pears up to 6″ tall and several feet wide. Terminal joint length: mostly 8–10″; terminal joint width: mostly 7–10″. Usually 1–4 spines per areole. Flowers waxy yellow to orange or red; 2–4″ long and wide.

Habitat Sandy or gravelly soils of plains, valleys, hillsides, and ridges in desert grasslands, deserts, pinyon-juniper woodlands, oak woodlands, and chaparral.

Range Southern Nevada, southwestern Utah, southern California, Arizona, southern New Mexico, and western Texas. Mojave, Sonoran, and Chihuahuan deserts.

54

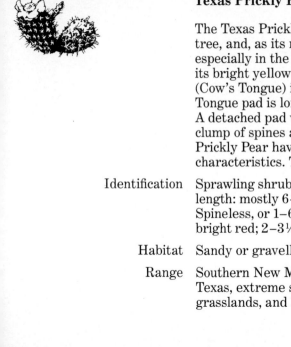

Texas Prickly Pear *Opuntia lindheimeri*

The Texas Prickly Pear can be a sprawling shrub or a small tree, and, as its name implies, it is found mostly in Texas—especially in the Laredo region. It is easily recognized by its bright yellow spines and green pads. Var. *linguiformis* (Cow's Tongue) is often used as an ornamental. The Cow's Tongue pad is long, narrow, and up to three feet long. A detached pad will root easily, quickly forming a massive clump of spines and pads. Several other varieties of Texas Prickly Pear have been described, based on pad and spine characteristics. The flowers bloom in May and June.

Identification   Sprawling shrub or small tree up to 10′ high. Terminal joint length: mostly 6–10″; terminal joint width: mostly 4½–8″. Spineless, or 1–6 spines per areole. Flowers waxy yellow to bright red; 2–3¼″ long; 2–4″ wide.

Habitat   Sandy or gravelly soils of plains and hillsides.

Range   Southern New Mexico, southcentral Oklahoma, southern Texas, extreme southwestern Louisiana, Great Plains grasslands, and Rio Grande plain. Chihuahuan Desert.

Coastal Prickly Pear *Opuntia stricta*

The Caribbean Islands and the West Indies are the natural home for the Coastal Prickly Pear. It was probably brought to the United States by boats sailing from the Caribbean, and a good spot to see this cactus is near the entrance to Galveston Bay. Also introduced to Australia, the Coastal Prickly Pear took over millions of acres of agricultural and grazing lands there before it was recently brought under control. Two varieties of Coastal Prickly Pear have been described: var. *stricta,* which is usually spineless, and var. *dillenii,* which has one to 11 spines per areole. The Coastal Prickly Pear blooms from May to July.

Identification
: Usually sprawling shrub up to 2′ tall and several feet wide. Terminal joint length: mostly 4–10″; terminal joint width: mostly 3–6″. 0–11 spines per areole. Flowers yellow; 2–2½″ long and wide.

Habitat
: Sandy soils of coastal regions and the eastern deciduous forest.

Range
: Gulf Coast region of Texas, southern Louisiana, coastal regions of Florida, southwestern South Carolina, and Caribbean tropical forest.

Pancake Prickly Pear *Opuntia chlorotica*

The pads of this prickly pear are almost perfectly round, giving rise to its common name. It is usually found growing on very steep hillsides in mountainous terrain and is widespread throughout much of the Southwest. The Pancake Prickly Pear is an erect shrub or small tree, and its areoles contain numerous yellow glochids and several golden spines. This prickly pear makes a very attractive ornamental. It blooms in May.

Identification Erect shrub or small tree up to 6′ tall. Terminal joint length: 6–8″; terminal joint width: 5–7″. 1–6 spines. Flowers light yellow; 1–1¼″ long; 1½–2½″ wide.

Habitat Mostly found on steep rocky slopes or, rarely, flats of deserts, desert grasslands, oak woodlands, chaparral, and pinyon-juniper woodlands.

Range Southern Nevada, southwestern Utah, southern California, northwestern and southern Arizona, and southwestern New Mexico. Mojave and Sonoran deserts.

Saguaro *Carnegiea gigantea*

These stately giants dominate the landscape of the Arizona desert, inspiring awe in many first visitors. The Saguaro provides food and habitat for many desert animals, such as the white-winged dove, the Gila woodpecker, the cactus wren, and the elf owl. The Baboquivari Indians (Papago) pick the fruit to make juice. A Saguaro grows very slowly at first, and you can get a very rough estimate of its age by counting the barely discernible constrictions and swellings on the stem. These desert guardians reach 50 feet high and may live up to 200 years. Their blossoms are the state flower of Arizona. The flowers, which are nocturnal and pollinated primarily by bats, bloom in May and June.

Identification Stems treelike and not branching for several years; length: 9–50′; width: 1–2′. 15–30 spines. Flowers white; up to 5½″ long; 2–2½″ wide.

Habitat Gravelly soils on hillsides, benches, and valleys in the desert.

Range Near the Colorado River in California, and east to southwestern Arizona. Sonoran Desert.

Barbed-wire Cactus *Acanthocereus pentagonus*

The Barbed-wire Cactus is a tropical, frost-sensitive cactus that barely enters the United States. It is often used in cultivation throughout Florida. The stems are weak, so the plants sprawl through other vegetation, making them difficult to see. In Texas, the Barbed-wire Cactus may form thickets so dense that it is difficult to walk through the stands. This "cereus" has three prominent ribs and very large, beautiful, white nocturnal flowers. It blooms from May to July.

Identification   Stems weak, sprawling to arching, bending at 3 different angles; length: up to 23′; width: 1–2″. 4–7 radial spines; 1–4 central spines. Flowers white to greenish white; 7–10″ long; 4″ wide.

Habitat   Sandy soils in coastal bottomlands.

Range   Southern tip of Texas, and southern Florida to the Florida Keys.

Organ Pipe Cactus *Lemaireocereus thurberi*

This cactus branches at the base, giving the stems the appearance of organ pipes. Since these sentinels of the desert are very sensitive to severe winter frosts, they are found only in the warmest parts of the Sonoran Desert. They do occur in extreme southern Arizona, where they are celebrated at Organ Pipe Cactus National Monument. The natives of Mexico make the large, delicious fruit into a candy they call *pitahaya dulce*. The nocturnal flowers are beautiful, and often attract bats. They bloom from June to September.

Identification Stems treelike, branching, and column-shaped; total length: 10–24′; total width: 6½–20′. 10–20 spines. Flowers lavender; up to 3″ long; 2–2½″ wide.

Habitat Gravelly or sandy soils on hillsides, and valleys in the desert.

Range Southwestern Arizona in and near Organ Pipe Cactus National Monument. Sonoran Desert.

Sprawling Cactus *Bergerocactus emoryi*

The bright yellow patches on the many-branching stems of this oceanside dweller are conspicuous. The Sprawling Cactus is most abundant in northern Baja California, and it enters the United States in the San Diego region. It is also found on Santa Catalina and San Clemente islands. Its nocturnal flowers are bright yellow, delicate, and attractive to view, but they have a mildly disagreeable odor. They bloom from April to September.

Identification Stems sprawling, and forming large colonies; length: 12–24″; total width: several feet. 20–30 spines, glistening yellow. Flowers bright yellow; 1½–1¾″ long; 1¼–1¾″ wide.

Habitat Sandy soils along the coast in the chaparral.

Range Extreme southwestern California.

Night-blooming Cereus *Peniocereus greggii*

This cactus usually grows in a mesquite, ironwood, palo verde, or other shrub that provides support and shade. It has the appearance of dead sticks and is uncommon throughout its range, making it very difficult to find. The white, showy, nocturnal flowers are large and extremely fragrant; their odor can be detected almost a third of a mile away. These make them so horticulturally desirable that they are subject to poaching by some cactophiles. The blooms appear from late May through June.

Identification   Stems inconspicuous, slender, ribbed, and mostly erect; length: 1–6′; width: ½″. 11–13 small spines. Flowers white; 6–8″ long; 2–3″ wide.

Habitat   Washes and bottomlands of deserts.

Range   Southern Arizona, southwestern New Mexico, and southwestern Texas. Sonoran and Chihuahuan deserts.

Claret-cup Cactus *Echinocereus triglochidiatus*

This wide-ranging cactus also goes by the names
Strawberry Cactus and King's Crown Cactus. A very
beautiful plant with long-lasting, waxy, glistening scarlet
flowers, the Claret-cup Cactus is a favorite among desert
landscapers. Some older specimens may have several
hundred stems. This species covers a diverse assemblage
of plants, and up to eight different varieties have been
recognized. Most of the varieties are distinguished by
stem, spine, and flower characteristics. The Claret-cup
Cactus blooms from May through June.

Identification   Stems globe- to cylinder-shaped; length: 3–17″; width:
2½–5″. 2–9 radial spines; 0–1 central spines, round to
angular, straight, or curved. Flowers scarlet with fuchsia
filaments and chartreuse stigmas; 2–2¾″ long; 1–1½″ wide.

Habitat   Rocky, gravelly, and sandy soils of the deserts, desert
grasslands, chaparral, oak woodlands, pinyon-juniper
woodlands, and lower montane forests.

Range   Southeastern California east to New Mexico, Colorado, and
southwestern Texas. Mojave and Great Basin deserts.

Fendler's Hedgehog Cactus *Echinocereus fendleri*

It is surprising to see such a small cactus produce such large and beautiful flowers. The purple flowers and the single, often variegated, straight or curving central spine are characteristic of this species. Three varieties are recognized: var. *fendleri,* which has an upward curving central spine; var. *rectispinus,* which has a straight central spine; and var. *kuenzleri,* which has no central spine and is protected by federal law. The Fendler's Hedgehog Cactus blooms from April to June.

Identification 1–5 stems, oval to cylinder-shaped; length: mostly 3–8″; width: 1½–2½″. 5–8 radial spines; 0–1 central spines. Flowers violet-purple; 2–2½″ long and wide.

Habitat Gravelly to sandy soils on hillsides or flats of deserts, grasslands, pinyon-juniper woodlands, and montane forests.

Range Southeastern Utah, eastern Arizona, southwestern Colorado, New Mexico and southwestern Texas. Sonoran, Great Basin, and Chihuahuan deserts.

Engelmann's Hedgehog Cactus *Echinocereus engelmannii*

Engelmann's is one of the most common hedgehog cacti found in the southwestern deserts. Its purple to magenta flowers and four well-armed central spines help to identify it. Nine varieties are recognized, based on stem size, central spine characteristics, and flower size. One of the most conspicuous and exceptional varieties is var. *nichollii*, which has golden yellow spines and tall slender stems. *E. engelmanii* blooms in April and May.

Identification Stems forming dense clumps up to 2′ high and 3′ wide; cylinder-shaped. 5–11 radial spines; 4 central spines. Flowers purple to magenta; 2–3″ long and wide.

Habitat Rocky, gravelly, or sandy hillsides and flats in deserts, desert grasslands, chaparral, pinyon-juniper woodlands, and montane forests.

Range Southern California, southern Nevada, southern Utah, and Arizona. Sonoran, Mojave, and Great Basin deserts.

Pitaya *Echinocereus enneacanthus*

The Pitaya usually grows in Texas near the Rio Grande and is especially common in Big Bend National Park. This cactus forms mounds of up to 100 soft, wrinkled stems. When it is covered with large purple flowers, it is one of the most striking of all the hedgehog cacti. The greenish brown fruits are edible and have a flavor similar to that of strawberries. Several varieties of Pitaya have been described, and many of them hybridize with each other. The Pitaya blooms in April and May.

Identification 5–100 stems, cylinder-shaped; length: 5–25″; width: 1½–4″. Forms mounds up to 8″ high and 4″ wide. 7–11 radial spines; 1 central spine. Flowers purple; 2–3″ long and wide.

Habitat Rocky and gravelly soils of limestone origin on hills and flats.

Range Southern and southwestern Texas. Chihuahuan Desert.

Strawberry Cactus *Echinocereus stramineus*

The Strawberry Cactus forms huge, domelike mounds with spines that look like straw. It grows best on dry hills and ledges of limestone. When in bloom, this magnificent cactus produces many large, showy, purple-red flowers with flaming red filaments, golden-yellow anthers, and bright green stigma lobes. The ripened fruits taste like fresh strawberries. The Strawberry Cactus is common in the Franklin Mountains near El Paso, Texas. It blooms in April.

Identification Stems cylinder-shaped. Forms mounds of up to 350 stems; mound up to 12″ high; up to 3–4″ wide. 7–13 radial spines; 2–4 central spines, straight or curved. Flowers 4–5″ long; 3–4″ wide.

Habitat Rocky or gravelly hillsides and ledges.

Range Southcentral New Mexico to southwestern Texas. Chihuahuan Desert.

Texas Rainbow Cactus *Echinocereus dasyacanthus*

The Texas Rainbow Cactus is well protected from the harsh elements by a thick covering of spines. In addition to protecting the cactus from being eaten, these pale spines reflect light and heat; they are dense enough to keep moist air emitted by the stem near the surface, retarding water loss. Each year's growth of spines may be a different color (white, yellow, or tan), giving the cactus a tidy, banded appearance. This cactus always has large, showy flowers, varying from waxy yellow to brilliant red, and spines that spread in all directions. Several different varieties have been described. It blooms in April.

Identification   Stems oval to cylinder-shaped; length: mostly 10–12″; width: 3–4″. 15–25 radial spines; 2–5 central spines, spreading in all directions. Flowers waxy yellow to bright red; 3–6″ long and wide.

Habitat   Rocky or gravelly hills and flats in desert grasslands.

Range   Southeastern Arizona, southern New Mexico, and southwestern Texas. Sonoran and Chihuahuan deserts.

Sonoran Rainbow Cactus *Echinocereus rigidissimus*

In appearance, this Sonoran desert-dweller is much like
E. dasyacanthus (Texas Rainbow Cactus); however, there
are some important differences. The Sonoran Rainbow
Cactus has no central spines, and its flower petals are thin
and fragile at the base while the Texas Rainbow Cactus has
two to five central spines, and its flower petals are woolly
at the base. The striking red and white horizontal bands
of spines and radiant magenta flowers with white throats
make the Sonoran Rainbow Cactus a favorite among
collectors. However, it is no longer common, and collecting
it is illegal. It blooms in May.

Identification   Stems mostly solitary, globe- to cylinder-shaped; length:
5–7"; width: 2–4". 6–7 radial spines; no central spines.
Flowers magenta; 2¼–3¼" long and wide.

Habitat   Rocky hillsides of limestone origin in desert grasslands.

Range   Southwestern New Mexico and southeastern Arizona.

Purple Candle *Echinocereus reichenbachii*

The Purple Candle is also known as the Lace Cactus for its lacelike spines. The easternmost of the *Echinocereus,* it is especially easy to find in the Wichita and Glass mountains of western Oklahoma. If the habitat is correct, hundreds of plants may cover the hillsides. Many different varieties have been described, mostly based on the presence or absence of central spines, radial-spine number, and color. The large, delicate flowers are some of the most attractive in the cactus family. The Purple Candle blooms in May and June.

Identification Stems solitary or forming large clumps, oval to cylinder-shaped; length: 3–10″; width: 2–2¼″. 12–33 radial spines; 0–2 central spines. Flowers purple or rose-pink with cream anthers; ¾–2¼″ long; 2–3″ wide.

Habitat Soils of limestone and gypsum on hillsides and flats in the grasslands and near the Rio Grande.

Range Southeastern Colorado, eastern New Mexico, central and western Oklahoma, and Texas.

Green-flowered Torch Cactus *Echinocereus viridiflorus*

The Green-flowered Torch Cactus is the most northerly of the *Echinocerei* genus and has never been found west of the Rocky Mountains. It thrives in the mountain foothills, Great Plains grasslands, and desert grasslands. Several varieties have been described, based on stem characteristics, spine color, and flower color. The Green-flowered Torch Cactus blooms in late May and early June.

Identification Stems solitary or clumping, oval to cylinder-shaped; length: 1–8″; width: 1–3″. 12–22 radial spines; 0–3 central spines. Flowers lemon- to straw-yellow to yellowish green; ¾–1″ long and wide.

Habitat Rocky or gravelly soils on hillsides and flats in deserts, grasslands, and desert grasslands.

Range Southwestern South Dakota, south to eastern Wyoming, eastern Colorado, and eastern New Mexico south to the Big Bend region of Texas.

Green-flowered Pitaya *Echinocereus chloranthus*

Its tall, slender stems and red, red and white, or brown variegated spines make the Green-flowered Pitaya a very handsome species. Two varieties are recognized: var. *chloranthus,* which has 13 to 22 radial spines, and var. *neocapillus* which has 30 to 38 radial spines. Only *neocapillus* has long, white, flexible, hairlike spines on the juvenile plants. *E. russanthus,* a close relative found in the Big Bend region of Texas, has gorgeous pale pink to reddish brown flowers. The Green-flowered Pitaya blooms in June.

Identification
Mostly 1–2 stems, cylinder-shaped; length: 3–10″; width: 2½–3″. 13–38 radial spines; 5–10 central spines. Flowers green to yellow-green or brown; 1″ long and wide.

Habitat
Limestone hills and ridges in desert grasslands and the Chihuahuan Desert.

Range
Southcentral New Mexico south to near Marathon, Texas.

Peyote *Lophophora williamsii*

Peyote, Mescal, Dry Whiskey, Turnip Cactus, and White Mule are just a few of the common names used for this cactus. Since ancient times many different tribes of Indians have used Peyote for its hallucinatory effects. Several alkaloids that alter the nervous system are found in Peyote, the most important of which is mescaline. Although this spineless cactus often grows alone, it may be found in clusters of up to fifty. Overcollecting has made Peyote a very rare plant. It blooms from May to June.

Identification The areoles of this cactus contain white or yellowish wool. Stems are globe-shaped; length: up to 2″; width: up to 5″. No spines. Flowers small, delicate, mostly pale pink to white; ½–1¼″ long; ½–1″ wide.

Habitat Limestone hills and flats.

Range Southwestern and southern Texas. Chihuahuan Desert.

Compass Cactus *Ferocactus acanthodes*

This barrel cactus stands like a tall soldier protecting the surrounding landscape. *Ferocactus* means "wild" or "fierce" cactus, and some of these are indeed imposing, often standing over six feet tall. Because this cactus leans toward the south or southwest, where the heat is most extreme, it has come to be called Compass Cactus. Three varieties are usually recognized: var. *acanthodes,* which is found mostly in the Sonoran Desert of California; var. *lecontei,* which is found mostly in the Mojave Desert; and var. *eastwoodiae,* which hangs from desert cliffs. The Compass Cactus blooms from May through August.

Identification	Stems elongated and cylindrical; length: 3⅓–7′; width: 1–2′. 6–14 radial spines, up to 6″ long; 4 central spines, red to gray. Flowers organized in a circular pattern, brilliant yellowish red; ¾–1½″ long; 1½–2½″ wide.
Habitat	Rocky hillsides and canyon walls.
Range	Extreme southern Nevada, southwestern Utah, southern California, and western Arizona (Grand Canyon). Mojave and Sonoran deserts.

Fishhook Barrel Cactus *Ferocactus wislizeni*

This is the most common barrel cactus and one of the largest in the southwestern deserts, with some older cacti reaching eight feet tall. Candy Barrel is another name used for this massive plant because many of them were used—and destroyed—in the making of cactus candy. The Fishhook Barrel Cactus has also fallen prey to collecting for the purpose of desert landscaping; many of the old plants do not survive transplanting. In this species the lower central spine is strongly hooked, inspiring the name Fishhook. *F. wislizeni* blooms from late spring into October.

Identification   Stems barrel-shaped to columnar; length: 1½–8′; width: 1–2′. 12–21 radial spines, gray; 4 central spines, red, forming a cross. Flowers showy, orange-yellow; 2–3″ long; 1½–2½″ wide.

Habitat   Rocky hills and flats of deserts.

Range   Southern Arizona and New Mexico. Sonoran and Chihuahuan deserts.

Coville Barrel Cactus *Ferocactus covillei*

Organ Pipe Cactus National Monument in Arizona is the best place to see the Coville Barrel Cactus. Bright red spines only partially obscure the massive stem. This species has only one central spine, which is strongly curved to hooked. The Coville Barrel's purplish red flowers mature into glistening yellow fruits. This giant is also common on the Papago Indian Reservation, where old plants can reach eight feet high. The Coville Barrel Cactus blooms in August and September.

Identification Stems barrel-shaped to columnar; length: 1–8′; width: 1½–2′. 7–9 radial spines, red; 1 central spine, up to 4″ long, strongly curved to hooked. Flowers purplish red; up to 1½″ long; 1¾–2½″ wide.

Habitat Rocky to sandy soils of hillsides and grassy flats.

Range Organ Pipe Cactus National Monument and the surrounding area in Arizona. Sonoran Desert.

Turk's-head Barrel Cactus *Ferocactus hamatacanthus*

The Turk's-head Barrel Cactus, which grows most often in Mexico, is never found too many miles north of the Rio Grande. It is the barrel cactus that is most often seen in the Big Bend region, growing in the shelter of some large shrub. One of the most important ways to recognize this cactus is by the large size of its hooked spines compared to that of its stem. Two varieties are usually recognized: var. *hamatacanthus*, in which the central spine does not curve in and out, and var. *sinuatus*, in which it does. This species blooms in late spring.

Identification Stems oval to cylindrical; length: mostly 6–12″; width: mostly 3–6″. 8–20 radial spines; 4–8 central spines, the longest up to 4″, very strongly hooked. Flowers yellow with brilliant red bases; 2½–3″ long and wide.

Habitat Rocky to sandy soils in deserts and desert grasslands.

Range Southwest Texas, mostly near the Rio Grande, north to extreme southcentral New Mexico. Chihuahuan Desert.

Many-headed Barrel Cactus *Echinocactus polycephalus*

Massive, symmetrical, sphere-shaped stems with dense, radial, stout spines and woolly areoles make the Many-headed Barrel Cactus one of the most splendid cacti in the United States. A wonderful place to see it is in Death Valley National Monument, where it is often found growing on a rocky alluvial fan. Var. *polycephalus* resides in the Mojave Desert and has spines covered with short, fine hairs. Var. *xeranthemoides* dwells in the Navajoan Desert, and has spines that contain few or no hairs. *E. polycephalus* blooms in June.

Identification Stems in large clumps of up to 30, mounds up to 3' high; stem width: up to 1'. 6–8 radial spines, red or yellow; 4 central spines, red or yellow. Flowers yellow and tinged with pink; 2" long and wide.

Habitat Rocky cliffs and hillsides.

Range Southern Nevada, southeastern California, east to extreme southwestern Utah, south to northeastern and extreme southeastern Arizona. Mojave and Great Basin deserts.

Turk's-head Cactus *Echinocactus horizonthalonius*

Within its natural surroundings, the Turk's-head Cactus is a hardened desert dweller. However, this species usually does poorly when transplanted to desert gardens. Also called Eagle-claws, it is easily recognized by its cylindrical shape, rigid stem surface, and stout spines. The flowers are a glistening rose-red. The most common variety is *horizonthalonius,* which is found in the Chihuahuan Desert and has stems up to six inches tall. Var. *nicholii* is quite rare and federally protected; it has stems up to eighteen inches tall. The Turk's-head blooms from May to August.

Identification   Stems globe-shaped to columnar, becoming more columnar as it grows older; height: 6″; width: 4–6″. 6–9 radial spines, gray; 3–5 central spines, gray to black. Flowers rose-red; 2–2½″ long and wide.

Habitat   Rocky limestone soils of deserts.

Range   Near Tucson, Arizona, southeastern New Mexico, and southwestern Texas. Sonoran and Chihuahuan deserts.

Horse Crippler Cactus *Echinocactus texensis*

The bright green stems of this cactus hide in the grass, almost flat to the ground, making it easy to overlook and stumble upon. Due to the arrangement of its brilliant red spines, it can cause the pain indicated by its name. If you have the misfortune of backing a vehicle over this low-growing plant, it can easily blow out a tire. Devil's-head is another deserved name given for what many ranchers consider a dangerous pest and try to eradicate. One attractive aspect of the cactus is its luminous red fruit. The Horse Crippler Cactus blooms in late spring.

Identification   Flattened to dome-shaped stems; length: 4½–8″; width: up to 12″. 5–7 radial spines; 1 central spine, red, turned downward. Flowers scarlet at base, orange in center, and then pink to white at the tips; 2½″ long and wide.

Habitat   Limestone and sandy soils of flats, hillsides, and valleys in grassland habitats.

Range   Extreme southeastern New Mexico east to southern and western Texas, except the Texas panhandle.

Mesa Verde Cactus *Sclerocactus mesae-verdae*

This federally protected cactus was first discovered near the Mesa Verde cliffs. Its pale grayish-green stems and short, straw-colored spines are not particularly outstanding, but the cactus's rarity has made it a favorite among cactophiles. Overcollecting and the extreme difficulty of keeping these plants alive in a garden have contributed to that rarity. The Mesa Verde Cactus grows in some of the most arid and alkaline conditions imaginable. Its stems are very difficult to see on the badlands, especially when it is dry and the stems lose their moisture and shrivel down into the ground. It blooms from late April to early May.

Identification   Stems depressed globe-shaped to short cylindrical; length: mostly 1½–4″; width: 1½–3″. 8–12 radial spines; 0–1 central spine. Flowers cream or white to pale pink; ¾–1″ long; ½–1¼″ wide.

Habitat   Adobe clay hills and mesas.

Range   Extreme northwestern New Mexico and adjacent Colorado. Great Basin Desert.

Uintah Basin Cactus *Sclerocactus glaucus*

The Uintah Basin Cactus is one of the few species in its genus that usually do not have a hooked lower central spine. It grows well in rocky or clay soils, often under a saltbush or some other type of shrub. Federally protected, this cactus has a very limited distribution. Two of the biggest threats to its existence are overcollecting and destruction by off-road vehicles. The radiant pink flowers are quite spectacular. They bloom in early May.

Identification Stems mostly solitary, often glaucus, round to globe-shaped; length: 1½–2½"; width: 1½–2". 6–8 radial spines; 1–3 central spines. Flowers bright pink; 1¼–1½" long; 1½–2" wide.

Habitat Rocky and adobe soils on hills and mesas.

Range Northeastern Utah to northwestern Colorado.

Devil's-claw Cactus *Sclerocactus parviflorus*

The Devil's-claw Cactus is notoriously variable in stem and spine characteristics and flower color; many varieties have been described. It grows in areas from low desert to high woodland. Some stems may reach a foot in length, which is quite large for this group. Var. *parviflorus* is found mostly in the Navajoan Desert, while var. *intermedius* usually grows in the pinyon-juniper woodlands. Var. *terraecanyonae* resides at higher elevations. The Devil's-claw Cactus blooms from late April to June.

Identification   Stems solitary or clustered, mostly cylindrical; length: 3–12"; width: 4–6". 7–11 radial spines up to 2" long. 4–8 central spines, 1–3 hooked. Flowers white to pink, purple, or yellow; 1½–2" long; ¾–2¼" wide.

Habitat   Rocky or sandy soils of deserts and pinyon-juniper woodlands.

Range   Southeastern Utah, southwestern Colorado, northern Arizona, and northwestern New Mexico.

Great Basin Eagle-claw *Sclerocactus pubispinus*

The Great Basin Eagle-claw cactus resides in the Great Basin Desert, where winters are frigid and summers are scorching. Large populations of this cactus are rarely found, and it is well-concealed among the surrounding hills and mesas. Traits that help to identify this cactus are ribbonlike spines and fruits that open along two or three vertical slits. The spines of young plants are covered with soft, white hairs. Two varieties of this cactus are recognized: Var. *pubispinus,* which has bronze flowers, and var. *spinoisor,* which has rose to violet flowers. This cactus blooms in May.

Identification | Stems mostly solitary and depressed globe-shaped to oval; length: ½–4″; width: ¾–6″. 8–11 radial spines; mostly 1–3 central spines, white to red or black. Flowers bronze or rose to violet; 1–1½″ long and wide.

Habitat | Rocky calcareous soils in sagebrush and pinyon-juniper communities.

Range | Eastern Nevada and adjacent Utah. Great Basin Desert.

Whipple's Devil's-claw Cactus *Sclerocactus whipplei*

Petrified Forest National Park in Arizona is an excellent place to see this little barrel cactus. A flat upper-central spine and small yellow flowers are important characteristic features. Whipple's Devil's-claw Cactus is widespread throughout much of the Navajo and Hopi Indian reservations. Here the plants often look like mounds of dried grass and are quite a task to spot. This cactus blooms from late April to early May.

Identification Stems mostly solitary, oval to depressed globe-shaped; length: 1–3½″; width: 1½–2½″. 7–11 radial spines; 4 central spines, upper central one flat and lower one hooked. Flowers yellow; ¾–1″ long; 1–1¼″ wide.

Habitat Rocky hills and mesas.

Range Northeastern Arizona. Great Basin Desert.

Mojave Devil's-claw Cactus *Sclerocactus polyancistrus*

One of the tallest barrel cacti of the Mojave Desert, *S. polyancistrus* has gorgeous dense, variously oriented spines that are up to five inches long. The hooked, contrasting red and white central spines and magnificent rose-purple to magenta flowers make this species very easy to separate from the rest of the genus. Many of these cacti dwell in Death Valley National Monument, often growing on alluvial fans. Remember, while visiting a national park, monument, or any other public lands, only take pictures, not plants. This lovely cactus blooms in April and May.

Identification   Stems solitary and cylindrical; length: mostly 4–6″; width: 2–3″. 10–15 radial spines, white, up to 5″ long; 9–11 central spines, hooked, red and white. Flowers rose-purple to magenta; 2–2½″ long; mostly 2″ wide.

Habitat   Rocky soils of hillsides and canyons.

Range   Southeastern California and adjacent Nevada. Mojave Desert.

Mountain Cactus *Pediocactus simpsonii*

This hardy little cactus is found not in the desert but in the high, cool Rocky Mountains, at altitudes of up to 11,000 feet. The Mountain Cactus grows quite well in frigid temperatures and blowing snow as long as it is situated on a slope that is warm and sunny during the summer. Occasionally cristate specimens, which display abnormal shapes, are found. The Mountain Cactus blooms from early May to June.

Identification   Solitary, or clusters of round stems; length: 1–6″; width: 1¼–6″. Mostly 15–28 radial spines, white. 4–10 central spines, mostly reddish brown. Flowers white, pink, magenta, or yellow; ½–1¼″ long; ½–1¾″ wide.

Habitat   Rocky hills in pinyon-juniper woodlands, sagebrush communities, and montane forests.

Range   Eastern Washington and Oregon to Idaho, Montana, and western South Dakota; eastern Wyoming, Utah, Colorado, northeastern Arizona; and northern New Mexico.

Knowlton's Cactus *Pediocactus knowltonii*

Knowlton's Cactus is a rare, dwarf cactus that is found only on one hill near the New Mexico/Colorado border. It has the smallest range of any known cactus in the United States. Due to overcollecting, the population has plunged from several thousand plants to several hundred, prompting New Mexico to institute an intensive recovery plan for the species. The lack of central spines and the comblike arrangement of radial spines help distinguish Knowlton's Cactus as a member of the genus *Pediocactus*. Federally protected, this plant grows in humus soils among rounded river rock. Knowlton's Cactus blooms from late April to early May.

Identification Globe-shaped stems, often in clusters; length and width: ½–1″. 18–26 radial spines, comblike; 0 central spines. Flowers bright pink with yellow stamens and greenish white stigmas; ½″ long; ¾″ wide. The fruit is shaped like a top, which is characteristic of this genus.

Habitat Rocky soils in pinyon-juniper woodlands.

Range Northwestern New Mexico.

Brady's Cactus *Pediocactus bradyi*

Well camouflaged by its yellowish tan spines, Brady's Cactus is almost impossible to detect growing in Kaibab limestone flakes. This charming little cactus also goes by the name Marble Canyon Cactus, after the site where it was first discovered in the early 1960s. It is now a federally protected plant. Three other members of this genus are found near the Marble Canyon of the Colorado River: Paradine Cactus (*P. paradinei*), which has hairlike spines; Fickeisen Cactus (*P. peeblesianus* var. *fickeiseniae*), which has corky spines; and Gypsum Cactus (*P. sileri*), which has delicately fringed yellowish brown flowers. Brady's Cactus blooms from late March to early April.

Identification Stem length: 1¼–2½″; width: 1–1½″. 7–18 dense radial spines, white to tan; 0 central spines. Early blooming. Flowers delicate straw-yellow; ¾″ long; 1/2–1″ wide.

Habitat Slopes of Kaibab limestone.

Range Northcentral Arizona. Great Basin Desert.

Winkler's Cactus *Pediocactus winkleri*

Cottony areoles and delicate, satinlike flowers make this cactus a striking one. The flowers may be so large that they completely hide the tiny plant. Winkler's Cactus was first discovered in 1979 and is now protected by federal law. The extreme summer and winter temperatures in its range cause its stems to shrivel into the ground, making it almost impossible to find Winkler's Cactus during certain months. Despain's Cactus (*P. despainii*) is quite similar to Winkler's Cactus, but its areoles are not woolly. Off-road vehicles and cattle are the biggest threats to these two cacti. Both species bloom from late April to early May.

Identification The areoles of this cactus are rarely without wool. Stem length: 1–2¾"; width: 1–2". 9–11 radial spines, white to tan, and spreading downward, partially obscuring the stem; 0 central spines. Flowers pink to peach; ¾–1" long; ¾–1¼" wide.

Habitat Alkaline hills.

Range Southeastern Utah. Great Basin Desert.

Peebles's Cactus *Pediocactus peeblesianus*

Each cluster of spongy spines of the Peebles's Cactus is shaped much like a Maltese cross. Although this is a hardy little cactus, its population has been greatly reduced due to construction of both an interstate highway and a coal-fired generating power plant in its range. Off-road vehicles have also contributed to destruction of its habitat. The cactus is now federally protected. Fickeisen Cactus (*P. peeblesianus* var. *fickeiseniae*) is more widespread and has more radial spines (four to seven). Both varieties shrink below ground level after blooming in late April and early May.

Identification   Bluish gray stems; length and width: ¾–2¼". 4–5 spines, white to pale gray, spongy. Flowers cream to yellow; ½" long; ½–1" wide. Fruit top-shaped.

Habitat   Gravelly hills.

Range   Northcentral Arizona. Great Basin Desert.

Grama Grass Cactus *Toumeya papyracanthus*

Spotting this small, rarely seen cactus usually involves crawling on your hands and knees. Its central spines are papery and mimic dried grass leaves. The Grama Grass Cactus often grows in the empty centers of older clumps of blue grama grass. It is easier to find in spring, when the bell-shaped white flowers appear. Albuquerque's urban sprawl has destroyed some of the habitat for this miniature cactus, and abusive grazing practices are undoubtedly affecting the vigor of remaining populations. The Grama Grass Cactus blooms in early May.

Identification Stems are usually solitary and cylindrical; length: 1–3″; width: ½–¾″. 6–9 radial spines, rigid and white. 1–4 central spines, curved and papery. Flowers white, bell-shaped; ¾–1″ long; ¾–1″ wide.

Habitat Sandy soils in grasslands and pinyon-juniper woodlands.

Range A small area in northeastern Arizona. Central and southeastern New Mexico to extreme southwestern Texas.

Button Cactus *Epithelantha micromeris*

The brilliant red chile-shaped fruits are quite striking
against the delicate white spines of the Button Cactus.
This tiny cactus thrives in the thin limestone cracks of the
desert, even though occasionally it is so cramped for space
that its stems are distorted from their usual tidy, golf-ball
shape. Because it is a favorite among many cactophiles,
the Button Cactus has become overcollected in many areas.
A closely related species is Boke's Cactus (*E. bokei*), which
has a smoother spine covering, larger flowers, and is found
only in the Big Bend region of the United States and
Mexico. The Button Cactus blooms in June.

Identification Stems with a depressed apex and shaped like a golf ball;
length and width: 1–2¼". Delicate white or ashy gray
spines up to ¼" long. Minute white flowers, which develop
into showy, bright red fruits; ¼" long; ³⁄₁₆" wide.

Habitat Limestone rocks and soils in desert shrub communities.

Range Southeastern Arizona and southern New Mexico to
western Texas. Chihuahuan Desert.

Glory of Texas *Thelocactus bicolor*

Almost entirely a Mexican genus, *Thelocactus* is found only near the border of the United States. Two varieties are found in Texas: var. *schottii*, with variegated red and white spines, and var. *flavidispinus*, with straw-colored spines. The striking, luminous, satiny fuchsia flowers set this cactus apart from any other in the region. Texans are quite fortunate that it crosses the border to set up a home near the Rio Grande. The Glory of Texas blooms from April to September.

Identification   Stems oval to cylindrical; length: 3–5½″; width: 2–3″. 10–17 radial spines, white or straw-colored; 4 central spines, red and white or yellow. Flowers fuchsia; 2–2½″ long and wide.

Habitat   Rocky soils of mesquite woodlands, desert grasslands, and desert communities.

Range   Near the Rio Grande in Brewster and Starr counties, Texas. Chihuahuan Desert.

Neolloydia *Neolloydia conoidea*

Neolloydia is a northern extension of a species that grows mostly over a large area in Mexico. It is not common in the United States but is found in Big Bend National Park and near Sanderson, Texas, on private land. The most prominent features of this Mexican plant are distinct tubercles and dark green stems. The magenta flowers on the tiny stems look like large sombreros. This species blooms from late May to early June.

Identification	Stems solitary to many, oval to cylindrical; length: 3–4″; width: 1–2½″. 15–28 radial spines, white; mostly 4 central spines, brown to black. Flowers magenta to purple; approximately ¾″ long; 1½–2¼″ wide.
Habitat	Rocky limestone hills.
Range	Southwestern Texas. Chihuahuan Desert.

Early-bloomer Cactus *Echinomastus intertextus*

This intriguing little cactus is always one of the first to bloom in its region, usually in March before most wildflowers open. Two varieties are generally recognized. Var. *intertextus,* which usually grows in the desert grasslands, has spines that are appressed against the stem. Var. *dasycanthus,* which usually dwells in the Chihuahuan Desert, has spines that spread in various directions. The flowers of the Early-bloomer Cactus are waxy and pale salmon to white with striking, brilliant purple-red stigma lobes.

Identification Stems globe-shaped to cylindrical; length: 2–6"; width: 1½–3". 13–20 radial spines, spreading; 4 central spines, with 3 pointing upward. Flowers pale salmon to white; ½–1" long; 1–1¼" wide.

Habitat Hills and mountains in deserts and desert grasslands.

Range Southeastern Arizona east to southwestern and southcentral New Mexico; southwestern Texas. Chihuahuan Desert.

Pineapple Cactus *Echinomastus johnsonii*

Pink to reddish spines that protrude in all directions, completely obscuring the stem, give the Pineapple Cactus a very bristly appearance. These small barrels resemble elongated spiny sea urchins, as well as the fruits for which they are named. The purple to pink-purple or chartreuse flowers are very charming. *E. erectrocentrus* (Needle-spine Pineapple Cactus) is a close relative that resides in the Sonoran Desert and Organ Pipe Cactus National Monument. The Pineapple Cactus blooms in April.

Identification   Stems mostly solitary and cylindrical; length: 4–10″; width: 2–4″. 9–10 radial spines; 4–9 central spines, straight to curving. Flowers purple to pink-purple or chartreuse; ½–2½″ long; 2–8″ wide.

Habitat   Granitic soils.

Range   The Death Valley region of California east to extreme southern Nevada and extreme southwestern Utah and south to northwestern Arizona. Mojave Desert.

Fishhook Cactus *Ancistrocactus scheeri*

The Fishhook is another cactus that resides mostly in Mexico and is not found very far north of the Rio Grande. It is easy to recognize by its hooked lower-central spine and two upper spines that form a very striking "V". This cactus often grows hidden among shrubs and is very inconspicuous. Its waxy flowers range from dark green to yellowish green or golden. The region around Falcon Lake, Texas, is an excellent place to see this species. It blooms from September to March.

Identification | Stems solitary, elliptical to columnar; length: 3–7″; width: 2–3″. 13–25 radial spines; 3–4 central spines, pale gray. Flowers dark green to yellowish green or golden; approximately 1″ long; ½–¾″ wide.

Habitat | Grassy plains and hills.

Range | Southwestern Texas; south of Eagle Pass and mostly near the Rio Grande.

Wright's Fishhook Cactus *Ancistrocactus uncinatus* var. *wrightii*

The Wright's Fishhook Cactus is quite easily camouflaged; the spines look like dried blades of grass or dead sticks. Most cactus hunters feel fortunate to spot one of these rarely seen plants. Var. *uncinatus* grows in Mexico and differs from var. *wrightii* in seed form and spine characteristics. Wright's Fishhook Cactus is best recognized by its long, tan, fishhooked spines, funnel-shaped flowers, and brilliant red fruits. This species blooms from April to June.

Identification   Stems oval to cylindrical; length: 3–6″; width: 2–3½″. 7–10 radial spines; 1–4 central spines, up to 4″ long. Flowers brownish maroon; ¾–1½″ long; approximately 1″ wide.

Habitat   Limestone ledges, hillsides, and flats.

Range   Southcentral and southeastern New Mexico to southwestern Texas, mostly near the Rio Grande and Trans-Pecos region. Chihuahuan Desert.

Long Mamma *Coryphantha macromeris*

Big Bend National Park, Texas, and near Las Cruces, New Mexico, are excellent places to see the Long Mamma cactus. It may be found in the open or under a shrub or small tree. The plant is named for its long, soft tubercles. It is usually found in clusters, and its beautiful flowers range from soft pink to bright purple. Var. *runyonii* has shorter tubercles and is found near Brownsville, on the Rio Grande plain. The Long Mamma cactus blooms in August.

Identification Stems forming short columns; length: 2–6″; width: 2–3″. 9–15 radial spines; 4–6 central spines, reddish brown to black. Flowers pink to bright purple; about 2″ long; 1–2″ wide.

Habitat Mostly gravelly soils on hills and flats.

Range Southeastern New Mexico to western Texas. Chihuahuan Desert.

Needle Mulee *Coryphantha scheeri*

Spotting a Needle Mulee has always been a treat for any cactus lover because these plants are extremely rare and never found in large numbers in any one area. It is best recognized by its long, dark green tubercles and stout spines. Three varieties are recognized: var. *scheeri,* which has one central spine; var. *valida,* which has one to five central spines and is often found growing on desert grasslands; and var. *robustispina,* which has one hooked central spine and grows in the Sonoran Desert. This species blooms from June to July.

Identification   Stems usually solitary, mostly elliptical; length: 4–7″; width: 3–4″. 6–16 radial spines; 1–5 central spines. Flowers yellow, often with red streaks; 2–2½″ long; 2–3″ wide.

Habitat   Hillsides; flats and bottomlands of desert grasslands; or desert shrub communities.

Range   Southeastern Arizona east to southern New Mexico and south to southwestern Texas. Sonoran and Chihuahuan deserts.

Spiny Star *Coryphantha vivipara*

The Spiny Star cactus is the most variable species of this genus; therefore, many different varieties have been described. Most of the varieties are differentiated by stem and floral characteristics and spine numbers. This cactus has been found from western Texas north to Canada, and at elevations of 1,000 to 10,000 feet. It is best recognized by its green fruit, short tubercles, and fringed sepals. The charming flowers bloom from May to June.

Identification Stems solitary to numerous, depressed globe-shaped to cylindrical; length: ¾–6″; width: ¾–4″. 12–40 radial spines, 3–12 central spines. Flowers pink to dark purple and magenta, or straw-yellow; 1–2″ long and wide.

Habitat Various soils in deserts, grasslands, pinyon-juniper woodlands, sagebrush communities, and montane forests.

Range Southwestern Oregon, Montana, Wyoming, east to the Dakotas and western Minnesota; southeastern California, Nevada, Utah, Arizona, New Mexico, western Nebraska, western Kansas, Oklahoma, and northern and southwestern Texas; southcentral Canada.

Nipple Cactus *Coryphantha sulcata*

The Nipple Cactus grows in thickets or clumps of grass and is rarely seen in the open. It is found in wetter conditions than is the typical desert dweller. Its bright green stems often form clumps that are several feet across. The most striking feature of the Nipple Cactus is its greenish or golden yellow flowers with brilliant red throats. It is one of the most beautiful flowers in the cactus family. This cactus blooms from June to August.

Identification	Stems branched and forming clumps, spherical; length and width: 1½–5″. 6–8 radial spines; 1–3 central spines. Flowers greenish or golden yellow with red throats; 1½–2½″ long and wide.
Habitat	Limestone soils.
Range	Southcentral Texas.

Sea Urchin Cactus *Coryphantha echinus*

In this species, a stout central spine stands straight out, giving the cactus the appearance of a sea urchin. The Sea Urchin Cactus is well armed with spines and quite suited for the harsh conditions of desert life. Its waxy, sulphur-yellow flowers will catch the attention of any cactophile. The flowers open in the afternoon and last only a couple of hours. The Sea Urchin Cactus blooms from May to June.

Identification Stems mostly solitary but, rarely, forming large clumps, spherical to egg-shaped; length: 2–4″; width: 1¾–2½″. 16–26 radial spines, yellow to gray; 3–4 central spines, gray to red. Flowers sulphur-yellow; approximately 2″ long and wide.

Habitat Gravelly soils of limestone origin; hills and ledges in deserts and desert grasslands.

Range Southwestern Texas. Chihuahuan Desert.

Cob Cactus *Coryphantha tuberculosa*

The common name of this cactus comes from its tendency to shed the spines on its older tubercles, which become corky and appear dead, making the stem look like a corn cob. The Cob Cactus is often found under rocks or bushes, and grows best in limestone soils. *C. dasyacantha,* a similar cactus with smaller flowers, is usually found in soils originating from igneous rocks. The Cob Cactus blooms from April to June.

Identification	Stems solitary or in clumps, egg-shaped to cylindrical; length: 2–8″; width: 1–2″. 20–30 dense radial spines, white, obscuring the stem; 4–9 central spines, straw-yellow. Flowers pink to pale purple; ¾–1″ long; ¾–1½″ wide.
Habitat	Mostly in soils of limestone origin; ledges and hillsides of deserts and desert grasslands.
Range	Extreme southeastern Arizona, southern New Mexico, and southwestern Texas. Chihuahuan Desert.

Sneed's Escobaria *Coryphantha sneedii*

In older specimens, the many-branched stems of this cactus can be found in one-foot-wide clumps of up to 100 heads. Due to overcollecting, however, there are very few such old patriarchs left, and the species is now federally protected. Two varieties are recognized: var. *sneedii*, which has spines that are not bent downward and bears pink to pale rose flowers, and var. *leei*, which has spines bent downward and brownish pink flowers. Sneed's Escobaria blooms in May.

Identification   Stems cylindrical; length: 1–2¾"; width: ½–1". 25–35 radial spines, white; 6–9 central spines, white. Flowers pink; ½–¾" long and wide.

Habitat   Limestone ledges and hills.

Range   Franklin and Guadalupe mountains of New Mexico and Texas. Chihuahuan Desert.

Ball Cactus *Coryphantha missouriensis*

The Ball Cactus dwells mainly in the midwestern Plains
States, all the way from North Dakota to central Texas.
It grows quite well as long as it has some shade and sandy
soils. During the hot summer months, this cactus will often
dry out and shrink to ground level, but during the blooming
season it swells back up and is quite conspicuous, with its
greenish yellow, starlike flowers. Many varieties have been
described. The Ball Cactus blooms from April to May.

Identification Stems solitary or branching, mostly spherical; length
and width: 1–2½". 30–75 radial spines; 0–1 central spine,
very similar to the radial spines. Flowers greenish yellow;
1–2½" long and wide.

Habitat Well-drained soils in grassland and pinyon-juniper
woodland communities.

Range Central Idaho, Montana, Wyoming, east to North and
South Dakota; southcentral Utah, Arizona, Colorado,
western New Mexico; northern Nebraska south to Kansas,
Oklahoma, central Texas, and southwestern Arkansas.

Living Rock *Ariocarpus fissuratus*

This cactus truly lives up to its name. It is found growing flat against limestone rock fragments, making the plant difficult to distinguish from the rock. The stems are spineless and have a very tough outer skin. The Living Rock is a hardy desert dweller, growing where there is little rainfall and where temperatures often soar above 125°F. It blooms from late September to mid-October.

Identification Stems depressed cylindrical; triangular nipples radiate in a starlike pattern as viewed from above; stem surfaces crossed by numerous fissures; length: 1½–2″; width: up to 4″. Flowers white to magenta; 1¼–1¾″ long and wide.

Habitat Rocky limestone hills and ledges.

Range Big Bend region to extreme southern Texas. Chihuahuan Desert.

Nipple Cactus *Mammillaria heyderi*

This is the only species of cactus in the United States in which the stems contain a milklike juice; hence its common name. It is unwise to use this characteristic for identification, however, because introducing a wound may lead to infection and disfigurement. Since it cannot tolerate full sunlight, the Nipple Cactus usually grows in partial shade provided by a small tree, a shrub, or blades of grass. When last year's carmine-red fruits are present with this year's ring of flowers, it is truly a magnificent sight. Several varieties are recognized throughout the Southwest. The Nipple Cactus blooms in May.

Identification   Stems mostly solitary, low growing, and turban-shaped to subglobe-shaped; length: 2″; width: 3–6″ usually at ground level. 9–26 radial spines, white; 1 central spine. Tubercles subcone-shaped to subpyramid-shaped. Flowers white to pink; 1–1¼″ long and wide.

Habitat   Gravelly hills and flats in deserts and grasslands.

Range   Extreme southeastern Arizona east to southeastern New Mexico and south to southernmost Texas; southwestern Oklahoma. Chihuahuan Desert.

164

Golf Ball Pincushion *Mammillaria lasiacantha*

This cactus truly looks like a fuzzy, white, spined golf ball. The white to pink waxy flowers and the bright scarlet fruits are a delight to see. The Golf Ball Pincushion thrives in scorching temperatures, so it is usually found out in the open. It is easy to confuse this cactus with the Button Cactus (*Epithelantha micromeris*), since the two often grow together. The Button Cactus usually has a depressed top, while the Golf Ball Pincushion does not. This cactus blooms in May.

Identification Stems mostly solitary, rarely 2–3, ball-shaped; length and width: ¾–1½". Spines dense, 40–80 per areole, white. Flowers white to pink; ½" long and wide.

Habitat Limestone hills and benches in deserts and desert grasslands.

Range Extreme southeastern Arizona; southeastern New Mexico south to southwestern Texas. Chihuahuan Desert.

California Fishhook Cactus *Mammillaria dioica*

The California Fishhook Cactus is found mostly in Baja California and barely extends its range into southern California. There are two forms: One dwells along the coast, while another makes its home in the Sonoran Desert. This cactus benefits from some shade, so it is often found tucked beneath a cholla or a tall shrub. The delicate, waxy flowers range from white to yellow with green and purple midribs. The California Fishhook Cactus blooms during the winter months, from November to April.

Identification Stems often branching and forming clumps, cylindrical; length: 4–8″; width: 1½–2½″. 12–17 radial spines; 1–4 central spines, one hooked. Flowers white to yellow with green and purple midribs; ¾–1″ long and wide.

Habitat Gravelly or sandy soils on hillsides and along washes in deserts and chaparral communities.

Range Extreme southwestern California. Sonoran Desert.

Arizona Fishhook Cactus *Mammillaria microcarpa*

The solitary, hooked, dark-colored central spine gives this cactus its name. When in bloom, the charming lavender flowers form a circle near the apex of the stem. The Clustered Fishhook Cactus (*Mammillaria thornberi*), a close relative, is often found growing near the Arizona Fishhook Cactus. However, the Clustered Fishhook has narrower stems and red, rather than green, stigma lobes. The flowers of the Arizona Fishhook Cactus appear in June and after summer and fall rains.

Identification Stems solitary or branching and cylindrical; length: 3–6″; width: 1½–2″. 15–29 radial spines; 2 central spines, the principal one hooked. Flowers lavender with green stigma lobes; ¾–1¼″ long and wide.

Habitat Sandy and gravelly soils along canyons, alluvial fans, and flats in desert communities.

Range Southern and westcentral Arizona, west to the Whipple Mountains in California. Sonoran Desert.

Graham's Fishhook Cactus *Mammillaria grahamii*

The Graham's Fishhook Cactus is often found hiding under bushes or in clumps of grass. The white radial spines contrast sharply with the red to nearly black central spines, making this fishhook a very impressive plant. Two varieties are often recognized: var. *grahamii*, which has one hooked central spine, and var. *oliviae*, which has no hooked central spine. These two varieties sometimes interbreed. Graham's Fishhook Cactus blooms in July.

Identification Stems solitary or branched and oval to spherical; length: 2–4″; width: 1¾–4½″. 20–33 radial spines, white; 1–3 central spines, red to nearly black, straight, curving, or hooked. Flowers pink to rose-purple; ¾–1½″ long and wide.

Habitat Rocky soils of hills or flats in deserts and desert grasslands.

Range Southern Arizona and New Mexico to southwestern Texas. Sonoran and Chihuahuan deserts.

Wright's Fishhook Cactus *Mammillaria wrightii*

The Wright's Fishhook Cactus is a very rare plant of the foothills. It is often found growing under a shrub or in a clump of bunchgrass, and during the late summer through the winter it shrinks down to almost ground level. Because of this tendency and its rarity, it takes a very keen eye to spot a Wright's Fishhook. Two varieties are recognized: var. *wrightii* which has an average of thirteen radial spines per areole and is usually found at elevations above 5,000 feet, and var. *wilcoxii*, which has an average of twenty radial spines per areole and is usually found below 5,000 feet. The Wright's Fishhook Cactus blooms after summer rains.

Identification — Stems mostly solitary and globe-shaped; length: 1½–4″; width: 1½–3″. 8–30 radial spines; 1–7 central spines, curved or hooked. Flowers magenta; ¾–2″ long; ¾–3″ wide.

Habitat — Low hills in grassland communities.

Range — Southeastern Arizona to southwestern and southcentral New Mexico.

Corky Seed Fishhook Cactus *Mammillaria tetrancistra*

The seeds of this Fishhook Cactus contain a white corky tissue that is a helpful characteristic in identifying the plant. This cactus grows mostly in the Sonoran Desert, often under a shrub or small tree. The most conspicuous features of the Corky Seed Fishhook Cactus are the one to four hooked central spines that spread at various angles. The showy flowers are rose-pink to purple and bloom in June and after summer rains.

Identification   Stems solitary and oval to cylindrical; length: 3–6″; width: 1½–2½″. 30–50 radial spines; 1–4 principal central spines, hooked; 0–4 accessory central spines, straight. Flowers rose-pink to purple; 1–1¼″ long and wide.

Habitat   Sandy soils of hillsides, valleys, and flats in desert communities.

Range   Southern tip of Nevada and Washington County, Utah, to southeastern California and southwestern Arizona. Mojave and Sonoran deserts.

Guide to Genera

Cacti are grouped into closely related species called genera. Some of the general characteristics of each genus are described on these pages, and are important for identification.

Pereskia

Considered a last link between cacti and evergreens, this genus has broad, flat leaves up to 2¾" long and forms clambering vines. Its woody stems are only moderately succulent. *Pereskia* looks more like a thorny bush than a cactus. These cacti are found only in Florida and the Caribbean region.
Page 18

Opuntia

The *Opuntia* group is made up of chollas (left) and prickly pears (right). Its areoles have minutely barbed bristles called glochids, and most have spines. When the stems are young, they bear a fleshy leaf at the base of each areole.

Prickly pears have flat-jointed pads, while chollas have tall, cylindrical-jointed stems. This genus contains the largest number of species.
Pages 20–60

Cereus (Group)

This is a grouping of genera which includes *Carneyiea* (left), *Acanthocereus, Lemaireocereus, Bergocereus,* and *Peniocereus* (right). It is almost impossible to describe general characteristics for the variable members of this group. However, in all these genera the stem is 15–100 times longer than the diameter. The flowers of this group are nocturnal except in the genus *Bergocereus.*
Pages 62–70

Echinocereus
Hedgehog cacti are included in this genus. Stems may be solitary or form large mounds. Dense spines cover the plant surface. Members of this genus often have large, showy flowers. With these species, the flower bud breaks an irregular opening through the epidermis of the cactus and leaves a scar above a spine-bearing areole.
Pages 72–90

Lophophora
Peyote is the only member of this genus. Stems of this cactus are bluish green, globe- or depressed globe-shaped, and spineless. The flowers are pale pink, pinkish white, or white. Peyote is found only in Texas and Mexico.
Page 92

Ferocactus
The stems of cacti in this genus are ribbed, usually unbranched, and up to 8′ long. The fruit remains fleshy for several months. Large barrel cacti are included in this genus.
Pages 94–100

Echinocactus

This genus contains small barrel cacti which have stems that are branched or unbranched, and covered with heavy spines. Soon after maturity, the fruit of this cactus becomes dry, obscured by woolly hairs.
Pages 102–106

Sclerocactus

Members of this genus range in size from small barrel cacti to species that grow at ground level. These cacti usually have solitary, ribbed stems. The fruits are dry and either do not open to release their seeds or open along vertical slits. The central spines are usually hooked except in two rare species.
Pages 108–118

Pediocacactus

The stems of this genus are not ribbed and grow either solitary or clustered. Fruits are dry, and green to tan, and open up along a vertical slit. One cactus (*P. simpsonii* var. *simpsonii*) within this genus is widespread; other species are rare.
Pages 120–130

Epithelantha
These "button cacti" are small plants with short, globular, branching or unbranching stems that are ½–1″ in diameter. Spines are short (only ½–5/16″ long) and flowers are small (only 3/16–1/4″ long). Fruit is brilliant red when mature.
Page 132

Thelocactus
This genus has small, globular or cylindrical stems. The flower-bearing portion of the areole is narrow, and the length is three to several times its breadth. The spines range in color from red and white to yellow, and are clustered around the tubercle tip. Flowers are rose and very large. These cacti are only found in Texas and Mexico.
Page 134

Neolloydia
Members of this genus have stems that branch and form green clumps. The lower central spine is longer than the other central spines, and the fruit is dry and green. The flower-bearing part of these cacti are separated from the spine clusters. This cactus is only found in Texas and Mexico.
Page 136

Echinomastus

As in *Neolloydia,* the flower-bearing part of these cacti are separated from the spine clusters. The fruits are green, the stems are unbranched, and the lower central spine is shorter than the other central spines.
Pages 138–140

Ancistrocactus

These small, well-hidden barrel cacti have flowers that grow apart from the spine cluster. The tubercles are grooved, the lower central spines are hooked, and some radial spines may be hooked. The fruit is fleshy and brilliant red when mature.
Pages 142–144

Coryphantha

As in *Ancistrocactus,* the flower-bearing part of these cacti are apart from the spine clusters, and the tubercles are grooved. Spines are generally straight. Fruit is fleshy, and green or red when mature.
Pages 146–160

Ariocarpus
The "living rock" cacti stems have no ribs, and the tubercles are flattened and fissured on the upper side. The flowers range from pink to magenta to white. This cactus is only found in Texas and Mexico.
Page 162

Mammillaria
Members of this genus can be quite diverse, ranging from solitary plants to clustering groups. The flowers and fruits are implanted deeply between the tubercles. Flowers form on the side of the stem, often away from the growing stem apex. The tubercles are not grooved, but rather, in spiraling rows.
Pages 164–176

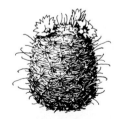

Glossary

Areole
The spot on a cactus that bears spines, leaves, or other growth.

Barbed
Having a barb like that of a fishhook.

Calyx
Collectively, the sepals of a flower.

Central spine
One or more spines in the central part of an areole. These are usually larger than the radial spines that grow around the edge of the areole; they are often hooked.

Cholla
A cactus, in the genus *Opuntia*, with short, cylindrical stems.

Cristate
Having a stem that shows an abnormal growth. Stems are often flattened and parallel.

Deciduous
Generally, refers to losing leaves in winter.

Depressed
More or less flattened in shape.

Family
A category in scientific classification that contains a group of related genera. Sometimes only one genus occurs in a family. Family names usually end in "aceae," as in Cactaceae, the cactus family.

Fruit
The fully developed ovary and associated parts of a flower that swell and ripen.

Genus
A category in scientific classification that contains a group of related species, or sometimes only a single species; plural, genera.

Glaucus
Having a whitish or bluish waxy coating, often called bloom, that is usually easily wiped off.

Glochid
A sharp, hairlike, barbed bristle found in areoles of the genus *Opuntia*.

Indicator plant
A plant that is associated with a certain habitat; its presence can often be a sign of general climatic and geological conditions.

Joint
One segment of a stem.

Ovary
The part of a pistil that contains the ovules, which will develop into seeds.

Ovule
An outgrowth of the ovary that develops into seeds.

Perianth parts
Collectively, the sepals and petals.

Petals
Inner whorl parts of the flower.
Usually brightly colored.

Pistil
The female portion of a flower,
consisting of the ovary, style,
and stigma.

Radial spine
One or more spines positioned
around the margin of an areole.
These are usually smaller than
the central spines and are
usually straight.

Root
The underground part of the main
axis of a plant; it helps anchor the
plant and absorbs water and
minerals from the soil.

Seed
A matured ovule.

Sepals
Outer whorl parts of the flower.
Often nearly the same color as the
petals in Cactaceae.

Species
A fundamental category of
scientific classification that
includes a population of organisms
that are capable of reproducing
among themselves but are
reproductively isolated from
other populations.

Spine
A sharp, needlelike structure that
is a modified leaf. In a cactus, it
grows out of an areole.

Sprawling
Lying on or leaning on, or over, an
object or another species.

Spreading
Having radial spines that grow
outward, as opposed to lying flat
against the surface of a stem.

Stamen
The male, pollen-bearing organ of
a flower, consisting of the filament
and the anther.

Succulent
A plant whose leaves or stems
are fleshy and juicy due to the
fact that they store water.
All members of Cactaceae
are succulents.

Truncate
Appearing squared at the tip
or base.

Tubercle
The stem projection bearing
the areole.

Variety
A subdivision of a species,
differing slightly but consistently
from the typical form and
occurring naturally.

Woolly
Plant covered with thick hairs.

Index

Numbers in italics refer to
plants mentioned as varieties
or similar species.

A

Acanthocereus pentagonus, 64
Ancistrocactus
  schoori, 142
  uncinatus var. *uncinatus, 144*
  uncinatus var. *wrightii, 144*
Ariocarpus fissuratus, 162

B

Ball Cactus, 160
Barbed-wire Cactus, 64
Barrel Cactus
  Coville, 98
  Fishhook, 96
  Many-headed, 102
  Turk's-head, 100
Beavertail Cactus, 42
Bergerocactus emoryi, 68
Boke's Cactus, *132*
Brady's Cactus, 124
Brittle Cactus, 40
Button Cactus, 132, *166*

C

Candy Barrel, 96
Carnegiea gigantea, 62
Cereus, Night-blooming, 70
Cholla
  Buckthorn, 22

Club, *34*
Devil, 34
Diamond, 36
Dog, *34*
Golden, 20
Jumping, 28
Rat-tail, 24
Silver, 20
Teddy-bear, 30
Tree, 26
Claret-cup Cactus, 72
Cob Cactus, 156
Compass Cactus, 94
Coryphantha
  dasyacantha, 156
  echinus, 154
  macromeris, 146
  macromeris var. *runyonii, 146*
  missouriensis, 160
  scheeri, 148
  scheeri var. *robustispina, 148*
  scheeri var. *scheeri , 148*
  scheeri var. *valida, 148*
  sneedii, 158
  sneedii var. *leei, 158*
  sneedii var. *sneedii, 158*
  sulcata, 152
  tuberculosa, 156
  vivipara, 150

Coville Barrel Cactus, 98
Cow's Tongue, 56
Creeping Cactus, 44

D

Desert Christmas Cactus, 32
Despain's Cactus, *126*
Devil's-claw Cactus, 112
  Mojave, 118
  Whipple's, 116
Devil's-head Cactus, 106
Dry Whiskey, 92

E

Eagle-Claw, Great Basin, 114
Eagle Claws, 104
Early-Bloomer Cactus, 138
Echinocactus
  horizonthalonius, 104
  horizonthalonius var.
  horizonthalonius, *104*
  horizonthalonius var. *nicholii*,
  104
  polycephalus, 102
  polycephalus var. *polycephalus*,
  102
  polycephalus var.
  xeranthemoides, *102*
  texensis, 106

Echinocereus
  chloranthus, 90
  chloranthus var. *chloranthus*, *90*
  chloranthus var. *neocapillus*, *90*
  dasyacanthus, 82
  engelmannii, 76
  engelmannii var. *nichollii*, *76*
  enneacanthus, 78
  fendleri, 74
  fendleri var. *fendleri*, *74*
  fendleri var. *kuenzleri*, *74*
  fendleri var. *rectispinus*, *74*
  reichenbachii, 86
  rigidissimus, 84
  russanthus, *90*
  stramineus, 80
  triglochidiatus, 72
  viridiflorus, 88
Echinomastus
  erectrocentrus, *140*
  intertextus, 138
  intertextus var. *dasyacanthus*, *138*
  intertextus var. *intertextus*, *138*
  johnsonii, 140
Epithelantha
  bokei, *132*
  micromeris, 132, *166*

F

Ferocactus
  acanthodes, 94
  acanthodes var. *acanthodes*, *94*
  acanthodes var. *eastwoodiae*, *94*
  acanthodes var. *lecontei*, *94*
  covillei, 98
  hamatacanthus, *100*
  hamatacanthus var.
  hamatacanthus, *100*
  hamatacanthus var. *sinuatus*,
  100
  wislizeni, 96
Fickeisen Cactus, *124*, *128*
Fishhook Barrel Cactus, 96
Fishhook Cactus, 142
  Arizona, 170
  California, 168
  Clustered, *170*
  Corky Seed, 176
  Graham's, 172
  Wright's, 144, 174

G

Glory of Texas, 134
Golf Ball Pincushion, 166
Grama Grass Cactus, 130
Gypsum Cactus, *124*

H
Hedgehog Cactus
  Engelmann's, 76
  Fendler's, 74
Horse Crippler Cactus, 106

I
Indian Fig, *48*

K
King's Crown Cactus, 72
Knowlton's Cactus, 122

L
Lemaireocereus thurberi, 66
Lemon vine, 18
Living Rock, 162
Long Mamma, 146
Lophophora williamsii, 92

M
Mammillaria
  dioica, 168
  grahamii, 172
  grahamii var. *grahamii*, *172*
  grahamii var. *oliviae*, *172*
  heyderi, 164
  lasiacantha, 166
  microcarpa, 170

tetrancistra, 176
thornberi, *170*
wrightii, 174
wrightii var. *wilcoxii*, *174*
wrightii var. *wrightii*, *174*
Many-headed Barrel Cactus, 102
Mesa Verde Cactus, 108
Mescal, 92
Mountain Cactus, 120

N
Needle Mulee, 148
Neolloydia, 136
Neolloydia conoidea, *136*
Nipple Cactus, 152, 164

O
Opuntia
  acanthocarpa, 22
  basilaris, 42
  bigelovii, 30
  chlorotica, 60
  clavata, *34*
  echinocarpa, 20
  echinocarpa var. *echinocarpa*, *20*
  echinocarpa var. *wolfii*, *20*
  engelmannii, 54
  ficus-indica, *48*
  fragilis, 40

fulgida, 28
humifusa, 46
imbricata, 26
loptocaulis, 32
lindheimeri, 56
lindheimeri var. *linguiformis*, *56*
littoralis, 48
macrocentra, 50
macrocentra var. *macrocentra*, *50*
macrocentra var. *santa rita*, *50*
phaeacantha, 52
polyacantha, 38
pusilla, 44
ramosissima, 36
schottii, *34*
spinosior, *26*
stanlyi, 34
stricta, 58
stricta var. *dillenii*, *58*
stricta var. *stricta*, *58*
whipplei, 24
whipplei var. *multigeniculata*, *24*
whipplei var. *viridiflora*, *24*
whipplei var. *whipplei*, *24*
Organ Pipe Cactus, 66

189

P

Paradine Cactus, *124*
Pediocactus
　bradyi, *124*
　despainii, *126*
　knowltonii, 122
　paradinei, *124*
　peeblesianus, 128
　peeblesianus var. *fickeiseniae*,
　124, *128*
　sileri, *124*
　simpsonii, 120
　winkleri, 126
Peebles's Cactus, 128
Peniocereus greggii, 70
Pereskia
　aculeata, 18
　grandiflora, *18*
Peyote, 92
Pineapple Cactus, 140
　Needlespine, *140*
Pitaya, 78
　Green-flowered, 90
Prickly Pear
　Coastal, 58
　Eastern, 46
　Engelmann, 54
　New Mexico, 52
　Pancake, 60

Plains, 38
Purple, 50
Sprawling, 48
Texas, 56
Purple Candle, 86

S

Saguaro, 62
Sclerocactus
　glaucus, 110
　mesae-verdae, 108
　parviflorus, 112
　parviflorus var. *intermedius*, 112
　parviflorus var. *parviflorus*, 112
　parviflorus var. *terraecanyonae*,
　112
　polyancistrus, 118
　pubispinus, 114
　pubispinus var. *pubispinus*, 114
　pubispinus var. *spinoisor*, 114
　whipplei, 116
Sea Urchin Cactus, 154
Sneed's Escobaria, 158
Sonoran Rainbow Cactus, 84
Spiny Star, 150
Sprawling Cactus, 68
Strawberry Cactus, 72, 80

T

Texas Rainbow Cactus, 82
Thelocactus
　bicolor, 134
　bicolor var. *flavidispinus*, *134*
　bicolor var. *schottii*, *134*
Torch Cactus, Green-flowered, 88
Toumeya papyracanthus, 130
Turk's-head, 104
Turk's-head Barrel Cactus, 100
Turnip Cactus, 92

U

Uintah Basin Cactus, 110

W

White Mule, 92
Winkler's Cactus, 126

Credits

Photographers and illustrators hold copyrights to their works.

Steven Brack (65, 129, 173)
Willard Clay/DEMBINSKY PHOTO ASSOC (67)
David J. Ferguson (25, 137)
Kenneth D. Heil (69, 73–77, 107, 119, 125, 135, 147, 151)
Larry Kimball/PHOTO/NATS (121)
John A. Lynch/PHOTO/NATS (47)
A. Peter Margosian/PHOTO/NATS (49, 169)
Ron Mossman (19, 59)
Elizabeth Neese (21, 23, 29, 39, 43, 61, 95, 109–113, 127)
Jo-ann Ordano/PHOTO/NATS (51, 63)
Stan Osolinski/DEMBINSKY PHOTO ASSOC (97)
Marv Poulson (37, 53, 117, 123, 141, 161, 177)
Thomas S. Sawyer (159)
David M. Schleser (27, 57, 81, 87, 89, 99, 115, 133, 149, 153, 155, 167)
Joy Spurr (41, 103)

Thomas K. Todsen (33)
Allan D. Zimmerman (45)
Dale and Marian Zimmerman (31, 35, 55, 71, 79, 83, 85, 91, 101, 105, 131, 139, 143, 145, 157, 163, 165, 171, 175)

Drawings by Edward Lam

Chanticleer Staff
Publisher: Andrew Stewart
Managing Editor: Barbara Sturm
Editor: Jane Mintzer Hoffman
Designer: Sheila Ross
Photo Editor: Timothy Allan
Production: Gretchen Bailey Wohlgemuth
Editorial Assistant: Kate Jacobs

Founding Publisher: Paul Steiner
Series Design: Massimo Vignelli

The NATIONAL AUDUBON SOCIETY is in the vanguard of the environmental movement. Its more than 600,000 members, 14 regional and state offices, extensive chapter networks in the United States and Latin America, and a professional staff of scientists, lobbyists, lawyers, policy analysts, and educators are fighting to save threatened ecosystems and to restore the natural balance that is critical to the quality of life on our planet. The society's system of sanctuaries protects more than a quarter-million acres of essential habitat and unique natural areas for birds, wild animals, and rare plant life.

The National Audubon Society publishes the award-winning *Audubon* magazine; *Audubon Activist,* a monthly newsjournal; *American Birds,* an ornithological journal; and *Audubon Adventures,* a children's nature newsletter. In addition, its award-winning Audubon television specials deal with a variety of environmental themes.

For more information, contact the National Audubon Society at 700 Broadway, New York, New York 10003. (212) 832-3200.